THE WHOLE EARTH SHALL CRY

GLORY

Iona prayers by Rev. George F. MacLeod

This book is dedicated in memory of
Lorna MacLeod

WILD GOOSE PUBLICATIONS

First Published 1985

OTHER RECENT PUBLICATIONS OF THE IONA COMMUNITY

Songs of The Incarnation — John Bell and Graham Maule
ISBN 0 9501351 8 6

The Iona Community Worship Book
ISBN 0 9501351 9 4

Through Wood and Nails — A Record and Cassette which includes
many of the Songs printed in the above books
and was recorded in Iona Abbey
No. 146/REC/S

Poverty, Chastity and Obedience — *A Vocation for Today*
ISBN 0 947988 00 9

Living Stones — *Unity Where It Matters*
Jim Maitland
ISBN 0 947988 02 5

What On Earth Is God Like? — *Three Bible Studies*
Jean C. Morrison
ISBN 0 947988 03 3

Several new publications are in preparation
—please enquire for details.

WILD GOOSE PUBLICATIONS

The wild goose is a Celtic symbol of the Holy Spirit.
It serves as the logo of Iona Community Publications.

The Abbey, Isle of Iona, by Oban, Argyll PA76 6SN

© The Iona Community
ISBN 0 947988 01 7

Made and printed in Great Britain by
Purnell and Sons (Book Production) Limited,
Member of the BPCC Group, Paulton, Bristol

THE MACLEOD CENTRE

Royalties from the sale of this book will go to the MacLeod Centre, which The Iona Community plans to build on Iona to replace the present Youth Camp.

It is intended that the MacLeod Centre will be an international ecumenical place of sharing with special provision for young people, for families, and for disabled people.

The MacLeod Centre will be open to people of any faith tradition or of none, and is being built as a sign of reconciliation for the future.

Details of the project and how it may be supported are obtainable from the Leader, Iona Community, Candlemakers' Hall, 36 Candlemaker Row, Edinburgh EH1 2QF (031 225 1135).

THE IONA COMMUNITY is an ecumenical community of men and women, clergy and lay, seeking new and radical ways of living the gospel in today's world. There are over 170 Members, with more than 800 Associate Members and 3000 Friends of the Iona Community spread throughout the world.

Though the historic island of Iona is its spiritual home, the Community's main work is in the world—particularly in what are regarded as difficult urban areas.

The Iona Community sees its primary task as being the discovery and making of community in a world divided: making peace in the midst of violence, discovering dignified and justly-rewarded work for all; witnessing to the power of God and the worth of each other.

Members share a common discipline—a five-fold rule of prayer and Bible-study, economic sharing, planning of time, meeting together, and working for peace and justice. Members live and work in different parts of the world—mainly in Britain, but some in Africa, New Zealand, India, Europe, Australia, Canada and America. The Community comes under the jurisdiction of the Church of Scotland, but its members are drawn from many denominations, Protestant and Roman Catholic.

The Community was founded in 1938 by Rev. Dr. George F. MacLeod of Govan (now Very Rev. Lord MacLeod of Fuinary) who was concerned by the church's lack of impact in working class communities at a time of high unemployment. He and his colleagues rebuilt the ruined medieval Abbey on Iona (a small island off the west coast of Scotland) as a sign of the necessary integration of worship and work, prayer and politics. The rebuilding was completed in 1967.

It was from Iona that St. Columba and his followers from Ireland launched a great missionary movement in the sixth century AD, leading to the evangelisation of much of Scotland and parts of Europe. Iona was renowned as an important centre of Celtic Christianity. The building of the Abbey was begun in the 13th Century by the Benedictines: it fell into disrepair after the Reformation.

The contemporary resident community lives and works in the restored Abbey throughout the year. On behalf of the Iona Community they maintain daily worship, offer hospitality to guests, and endeavour to practise a lifestyle of simplicity, responsibility and celebration. The Iona Community also has youth centres on Iona and Mull. Groups and individuals are welcome all the year round. On the mainland, the Community has a peace centre in Glasgow, publishes a quarterly newspaper *The Coracle*, supports a ministry to the unemployed and a network of community or 'Columban' houses aiding the work of churches in disadvantaged areas.

Further information regarding the programme of the residential centres may be had from The Abbey, Iona, Argyll PA76 6SN Telephone: (06817) 404.

Further information regarding the life and work of the Community may be had from The Iona Community, Pearce Institute, Govan, Glasgow G51 3UT Telephone: (041) 445 4561.

CONTENTS

Page No.

INTRODUCTION

George Fielden MacLeod, whose 90th birthday this book celebrates, is perhaps best known as a prophetic figure. His passionate calls for political and social justice, his tireless campaigning for nuclear disarmament and his action for the rebuilding of community—symbolised by the prophetic sign of the rebuilding of Iona Abbey—have deservedly made him one of the most noted churchmen of this century.

Perhaps less widely celebrated—but certainly no less important—is his peerless leadership of worship. To be in a seat at Iona Abbey, to be moved by the awesome oratory of a MacLeod sermon in full flood, to be led into the nearer presence of God by means of kaleidoscopic, imaginative prayer, is to be privileged and—more importantly—to be changed.

George MacLeod might well be described as a conservative radical. The urgent radicalism of his views on politics and peace spring not from modern sociological analysis, but from a profound sense of the holy at the heart of life. The theology is orthodox, Trinitarian, but hardly formal or static. Holiness, wholeness, health are held together by a deep personal piety and concern for individual people. The personal becomes political in a vision which pushes the parameters of theological orthodoxy, yet just remains within the creedal boundaries—Christ at the heart of the cosmos; Christ the light of the world—in all, through all; Christ the light energy in and through all matter. For George MacLeod the material is the vehicle of the spiritual and is therefore holy: if Christ is in all things, everything is every *blessed* thing, and the political as well as the personal comes under his sovereignty. The whole earth shall cry glory! It is a theology of incarnation and a theology of transfiguration, with a high view of the church. George's radicalism is therefore a matter of roots: and the roots are to be found in personal and public worship of a holy yet accessible God, who is in and through all things. In G. F. MacLeod the prophetic and the priestly come together in a unique way.

These prayers, then, come out of this context. Preparation for worship has always been, and remains, fundamental for George MacLeod, as all who have shared in leading worship with him will testify. Five hours preparation for a five minute prayer is by no means unusual.

The language of the prayers is evocative of the Celtic mysticism of Columban Iona. The profound spirituality, linked with deep reverence for the earth and the common things of life, so characteristic of Celtic Christianity, are reflected here: so also is the rich, imaginative language and unexpected phrase which lights up another aspect of the world.

The initial editing was done with painstaking and loving care by Brian Crosby, Warden of Iona Abbey from 1977–80 and now working with the Presbyterian Church of Canada in Mauritius. In continuing the editing process and bringing it to completion, I have followed Brian's guidelines.

The prayers in their original were urgent, scribbled, telegrammatic, embodied. They would be reworked and rewritten and fitted into new prayers, so that there might be many revisions of the same prayer. I have taken out dated historical references to avoid the need for footnotes, and have provided titles to identify each meditation. All of the prayers were used at some time or another as part of the regular worship of the Iona Community in Iona Abbey, during or after the rebuilding. The island—spiritual home of Celtic, Roman Catholic, Protestant and ecumenical traditions—is seldom far away. The photographs are therefore intended to be visual aids to assist meditation.

Thanks are due to Rosemary Beimers, Anna Briggs, Duncan and Marlene Finlayson, Ian and Kathy Galloway, Alice Gillan, Tom Gordon, Geoff Houghton, Michael Lee, Uist MacDonald, Mary Macgregor, Margaret Simpson, Don Stubbings, Jean and Raymond Young for help and encouragement in enabling this manuscript to see the light of day. It has indeed been for all concerned a labour of love.

Finally: these prayers and meditations are offered by the Iona Community as a gift to the Church at large, as an appropriate 90th birthday tribute to one of Scotland's greatest of churchmen.

Ron Ferguson,
Leader of the Iona Community

THE WHOLE EARTH SHALL CRY GLORY

Almighty God, Creator:
the morning is Yours, rising into fullness.
The summer is Yours, dipping into autumn.
Eternity is Yours, dipping into time.
The vibrant grasses, the scent of flowers, the lichen on the
    rocks, the tang of sea-weed,
All are Yours.
Gladly we live in this garden of Your creating.

But creation is not enough.
Always in the beauty, the foreshadowing of decay.
The lambs frolicking careless: so soon to be led off to
    slaughter.
Nature red and scarred as well as lush and green.
In the garden also:
always the thorn.
Creation is not enough.

Almighty God, Redeemer:
the sap of life in our bones and being is Yours,
lifting us to ecstasy.
But always in the beauty: the tang of sin, in our consciences.
The dry lichen of sins long dead, but seared upon our minds.
In the garden that is each of us, always the thorn.

Yet all are Yours as we yield them again to You.
Not only our lives that You have given are Yours:
but also our sins that You have taken.
Even our livid rebellions and putrid sins:
You have taken them all away
and nailed them to the Cross!
Our redemption is enough: and we are free.

Holy Spirit, Enlivener:
breathe on us, fill us with life anew.
In Your new creation, already upon us, breaking through,
    groaning and travailing,
but already breaking through,
breathe on us.

Till that day when night and autumn vanish:
and lambs grown sheep are no more slaughtered:
and even the thorn shall fade
and the whole earth shall cry Glory at the marriage feast of
  the Lamb.
In this new creation, already upon us,
fill us with life anew.

You are admitting us now into a wonderful communion,
the foretaste of that final feast.
Help us to put on the wedding garment of rejoicing
which is none of our fashioning
but Your gift to us alone.
By the glories of Your creation,
which we did not devise:
by the assurance of Your freeing us,
which we could not accomplish:
by the wind of Your spirit,
eddying down the centuries through these walls renewed:
whispering through our recaptured oneness,
fanning our faith to flame,
help us to put on the wedding garment.
So shall we go out into the world,
new created, new redeemed, and new enchained together:
to fight for Your kingdom
in our fallen world.

ETERNAL SEEPING THROUGH THE PHYSICAL

We come into Thy house, our home
once more to give thanks:
for earth and sea and sky in harmony of colour,
the air of the eternal seeping through the physical,
the everlasting glory dipping into time.
We praise Thee.

For nature resplendent:
growing beasts, mergent crops, singing birds,
and all the gayness of the green.
We bless Thee.

For swift running tides, resistant waves, Thy spirit on the
    waters,
the spirit of the inerrant will,
Striving with the currents that are also Thine.
We bless Thee.
O Lord: how marvellous are Thy works.
In majesty hast Thou created them.

As we look on man
we thank thee above all that Thou hast been mindful of us
in Jesus Christ, our Lord:
that even as man fell from Thy creation which was good,
so Thou didst send the Proper Man to restore in us the
    image:
that we find the road to harmony again in Him.
We praise Thee.
Yes: already vibrant with the everlasting,
we are enriched beyond the noblest works of nature.
That the spirit moves upon the turbulent waters of our lives:
We bless Thee.
Yes: that Thou dost honour each of us
with a flowing tide and also with resistant waves,
and that the waves only engulf when we lose our trust in
    Thee:
We give Thee manly thanks.

And that even Thou who hast set the stars upon their courses
hast also set each one of us within the orbit of Thy love.
The hairs of our head are numbered.
We give Thee humble praise.

By the awareness of Thy good creation round us,
by the intimations of Thy redemption in us,
by the pulsing sense of Thy spirit round about us and
    between us—
What else is left for us to do but to say sorry?
For our earthiness and our laziness:
our blindness and forgetting.
What else but to kneel when we see Thee hanging there,
bleeding there, but most certainly risen there
and waiting till we all get together there to take Thee down.
Give us life that we may be penitent.
Penitent that we may live.

THE GLORY IN THE GREY

Almighty God, Creator:
In these last days storm has assailed us.
Greyness has enveloped and mist surrounded
our going out and our coming in.
Now again Thy glory clarifies,
Thy light lifts up our hearts to Thee,
and night falls in peace.
But through mist and storm and sunshine,
the crops have ripened here
and vines of Spain have grown.
Thy constant care in all and everywhere is manifest.

Almighty God, Redeemer:
Even as with our bodies, so also with our souls.
Redeemer, Christ:
Sunshine and storm, mist and greyness
eddy round our inner lives.
But as we trace the pattern, looking back,
we know that both darkness and light have been of Thine
    ordaining
for our own soul's health.
Thy constant care in all, and everywhere,
is manifest.

Almighty God, Sustainer:
Sun behind all suns,
soul behind all souls,
everlasting reconciler of our whole beings:
Show to us in everything we touch and in everyone we meet
the continued assurance of Thy presence round us:
lest ever we should think Thee absent.
In all created things Thou art there.
In every friend we have
the sunshine of Thy presence is shown forth.

In every enemy that seems to cross our path,
Thou art there within the cloud
to challenge us to love.
Show to us the glory in the grey.
Awake for us Thy presence in the very storm
till all our joys are seen as Thee
and all our trivial tasks emerge as priestly sacraments
in the universal temple of Thy love.

Of ourselves we cannot see this. Sure physician give us sight.
Of ourselves we cannot act. Patient lover give us love:
till every shower of rain speaks of Thy forgiveness:
till every storm assures us that we company with Thee:
and every move of light and shadow speaks of grave and
    resurrection:
to assure us that we cannot die:
Thou creating, redeeming and sustaining God.

MAN IS MADE TO RISE

CHRIST ABOVE US: CHRIST BENEATH US:
CHRIST BESIDE US: CHRIST WITHIN US.
Invisible we see You, Christ above us.
With earthly eyes we see above us, clouds or sunshine,
   grey or bright.
But with the eye of faith, we know You reign:
        instinct in the sun ray,
        speaking in the storm,
        warming and moving all Creation, Christ above
        us.

We do not see all things subject unto You.
But we know that man is made to rise.
Already exalted, already honoured, even now our citizenship
is in heaven, Christ above us, invisible we see You.

Invisible we see You, Christ beneath us.
With earthly eyes we see beneath us stones and dust
and dross, fit subjects for the analyst's table.
But with the eye of faith, we know You uphold.
In You all things consist and hang together:
        The very atom is light energy,
        The grass is vibrant,
        The rocks pulsate.

All is in flux; turn but a stone and an angel moves.
Underneath are the everlasting arms.
Unknowable we know You, Christ beneath us.

Inapprehensible we know You, Christ beside us.
With earthly eyes we see men and women, exuberant or
   dull, tall or small.
But with the eye of faith, we know You dwell in each.
You are imprisoned in the lecherous, the dope fiend and
the drunk, dark in the dungeon, but You are there.

You are released, resplendent, in the loving mother,
the dutiful daughter, the passionate bride,
and in every sacrificial soul.
Inapprehensible we know You, Christ beside us.

Intangible, we touch You, Christ within us.
With earthly eyes we see ourselves, dust of the dust, earth
of the earth; fit subject, at the last, for the analyst's
table. But with the eye of faith, we know ourselves all girt
about of eternal stuff,
> our minds capable of Divinity,
> our bodies groaning, waiting for the revealing,
> our souls redeemed, renewed.
Intangible we touch You, Christ within us.

Christ above us, beneath us, beside us, within us, what need
have we for temples made with hands? . . . save as a passing
place in which to gather and adore and be abased?
We are Your living temple, by grace alone we are Your living
body, the only hope of Clarity for the world—Blessed
be Your name for Your glorious Gospel.

IT IS SO.

AWAKE OUT OF SLEEP!

It is high time to awake out of sleep;
for our salvation is nearer at hand than when first we
  believed.

We confess that we sleep
when we think the world is as it always was.
It is high time to awake
to the truth that Jesus has come.
His summons is urgent in our midst.
Nearer than we know He is coming in judgement.
He might come in judgement this Christmas.

We confess that we sleep
when we think that power is still of this world.
It is high time to awake
to the truth that His power alone is working permanently.
All the civilizations builded in scorn of His power
are as if they had never been.
And our civilization with them will equally go down.

Nearer than we know
He will be seen coming in power.
He might come in power this Christmas.

We confess that we sleep
when we think that His glory is veiled.
He has been seen,
He has died,
He has risen,
He reigns.

It is high time to awake to the truth
that His glory is manifest
In all the deeds that sweeten,
in all the thoughts that help.
Nearer than we know
He will be seen coming in glory,
to exalt the humble and meek
and to cast down the mighty from their seats.
He might come in glory this Christmas.

And we . . . we accept the ways of this world and its
    judgements.
We accept the power of this world despite their obvious
    bankruptcy.
We accept the tinsel, the gold and the glare
despite their emptiness—
till with this world's eyes
we see Christmas coming as a carnival,
and not as a confusion of face.

Give us grace to wait in spiritual expectancy
His coming again to practice true humility,
to be exercised in the ways of real power,
to express His glory:
that, we may recognise the kingship of a cradle,
the royalty of being ruled,
the seniority of service:
So that should He come this Christmas,
His body bloody but His head crowned,
we would be found among those who worshipped
and not among those who would kill.
If these things would be:
it is high time to awake out of sleep.

THE COST OF A CHANGING DAY

Ever present God:
Everything is in Your hands.
You ordained everything; ordered everything.
You made all ages a preparation for the coming of Your Son.
You called your people out of Egypt to cradle Him.
Your prophets foretold Him, Son of David, infant of Mary.
And when the time was ripe He came:
Wielding the hammer,
treading the winepress,
tramping the earth,
contradicting the smooth,
giving hope to the sinners,
redeeming the world.

Ever present God:
Everything is still in Your hands.
Out of eternity You have called each one of us
into Your Church.
By the spirit of prophecy
You have awakened our souls to expectancy.
By most strange choosing
it is we You have named
to redeem the world by faith in You,
continuing Your incarnation.
Heavenly Father:

We acknowledge our unworthiness to be that continuing
    incarnation.
We sing of His birth in a stable,
but we hardly accept His presence in so rancid a place.
We rejoice that shepherds acclaimed Him at their work,
but we don't make our work the sort of place to meet Him.
We acknowledge His welcome by the wise men who had to
    change direction to find Him,
but we want to be wise without changing direction.

We are content to be humbled,
if we can keep our pride.
We are ready for the unexpected story,
so long as we can continue in our own expected way.

We don't want to be born again when we are old:
How can we possibly be born again when we are old?
Yet—

Take us O God and remake us.
Give us boldness to enter through the veil
that is His flesh: knowing in fullness of faith
that our hearts are cleansed from an evil conscience:
so that we may consider one another,
and provoke one another to good works,
and open our minds and hearts
to the meaning and the cost of a changing day.

SEND US AN ANGEL

Lord God: some of us are a little like the Shepherds;
just carrying on with our jobs . . . despite the
turbulence in the world scene.
Give us a message . . . send us an angel
that will start us seeking a new way of life.

Lord God: others of us are like the Wise Men from the east;
we can see the need of some power to come
and to give us direction:
but we don't know in which direction to go.
Give us the wisdom to see that it is not in physical power
that our salvation lies,
but in love and humility.

Lord God; a few of us are like Herod;
we don't want a new power to enter the world,
in case it might threaten our own power.
Give us the humility to be ready
for a quite new form of power:
to fit the dangerous age in which we live:
where atomic power is beyond our capacity to control.

We ask You to make us expectant,
instead of planners:
We ask You to make us seekers,
rather than know-alls.

We ask You for grace
so that we are ready to receive.
We ask You for humility
so that we are prepared to accept Your way of doing things.
We ask You for faith, and faith is a gift,
really to believe;
that, in this dark day for our land, we can accept the gift of
    Christmas:
and bring our wealth as a land to serve the Christ;
to bring our incense to worship Him:
and our myrrh, the symbol of burial,
to be ready to die for Him.

Thus we shall be able
to receive the gift of love and light and life,
when Christmas Day shall dawn.

NEARER TO THAT EXPECTANCY

Let us pray for shepherds: all who carry on their work in
   cold and sleet:
those burdened down in serving in our shops,
those soaked and cold in guarding our city,
all who in country field or city street and factory
tend the everlasting fire of sacrifice
that men may be housed and fed.
As Thou didst appear to shepherds who were amazed,
speak to all these that their work is holy.

Let us pray for wise men: all who in their science and studies
seek a star that will lead to harmony:
all who in their planning take long journeys of adventure
that others need not take them but may find rest:
all who have grown tired of being merely clever and seek
a simple solution in the paths of love.
As Thou didst appear to the wise men from the East
speak to all these that they may place their talents and their
gifts at Thy disposal.

Let us pray for the devout: all who find time to think of
   eternal things
lest temporal things become chaos:
all who linger in the house of God, knowing that He hears
and will answer:
all who pray for the sick as well as tending them
and intercede for the world instead of cursing it.
As Thou in the temple courts did appear to Anna and Simeon
speak to all these in fulfilment of their prayers.

We bless Thee for protection on our homes.
We praise Thee for all who have made true Christmas real to us
in the words they have spoken in our youth,
the things they have done for us in our pilgrimage.
May we be warm where there is bitterness
            be strong where there is doubt
            be patient where there is opposition.
So shall this advent bring folk nearer to that family that is
   in Thee;
And to that expectancy without which we cannot see the Lord.

SPEAK PEACE TO US

Lord Christ, who didst say to Thy disciples
Peace be unto you,
showing to them Thy pierced hands and broken side:
speak also to us,
locked in our fretfulness and doubts,
as we seek to know Thee risen and serene.
And, as we glimpse Thy hands and side,
remind us that Thou hast also walked
in the valley of our death.
Thou who art risen, and was humbled,
Thou who art serene, and whose heart was broken,
Thou who art everlasting, and hast known death for us:
Speak peace to us all.

Lord Christ we are not worthy of it.
We are such cowards, Lord.
Even as Thy disciples fled away
how often have we shrunk back or stood silent
when Thy name has been blasphemed.
Yet to them Thou didst speak peace.
Speak peace to us.

We are so unbelieving, Lord.
Even as Thy disciples called Thy resurrection foolish talk:
how often have we too tried to walk in the light of the sun,
but not in the light of everlasting life.
Yet to them Thou didst speak peace:
speak peace to us.

Even as they, despite their life renewed,
went back to the fishing:
we have felt the old life tugging at us
because of Thy difficult way.
But do Thou appear to us,
as Thou didst to them,
to fill our hearts with faith.
Forgive the sin that ever mingles,
even with our holiest things
and all wherein we have grieved Thy holy spirit.

Let Thy Resurrection light radiate all our worship:
by the power of the Holy Spirit.
Help us to know ourselves
as men and women who have been made new.
By that same power inspire us to walk
even as he walked:
that going on our way in faith and gladness
we may come at last to those things which eye hath not seen
    nor ear heard
but which Thou hast prepared for all them that truly love
    Thee
from the beginning of the world.

THE SPIRIT WHICH INVADES OUR HEARTS

Lord God, Creator:
it is so wonderful to know that You are forever creating:
creating us continually not just in our souls
not just in this house of stone
but in the bodies of each of us.

Lord Jesus:
        it is so wonderful to know of Your incarnation
        that You really came in the flesh,
        have walked where we walk,
        have felt what we feel:
        and that time and time again You could not get
           away to pray
        because of the pressures of everyday.
It is so wonderful to know that You came that we might find you
        in the pressure of life;
        we are released
        that You have been with us this day.

Lord Jesus:
        it is such anguish to know of Your cross;
        that You came to defeat the dirt in all the
           pressures
        to set at nought the harshness in our daily
           contacts,
        to obliterate our treacheries and our rawness—by
           Your love.
It is so wonderful to know of Your resurrection
        so that the cross is empty
        and all the dirt and harshness and rawness of
           today
        has been done away.

Lord Jesus:
        it is so wonderful to know of the spirit which You
           sent
        and which even now invades our hearts.
        By whose invading even now we know
        that our thinking, feeling and willing are made
           new.

BOUGHT BACK FROM THE PAWNSHOP OF DEATH

Christ have mercy.
You sit at the right hand of God
            Interpreter of truth,
            dispenser of gifts,
            advocate of sinners.
But we dodge the truth
doubt the gifts
discount any need of Your advocacy.
Have mercy.

We glory in Your creation, Father:
            In Your buying us back from the pawnshop of
                death: Christ.
            In Your supporting: Spirit of uplift.
But we do not make this clear to men on earth.
Rather do we grossly defile Your creation,
            lightly presume on what it cost You to win us back
            till we assume it is our zest and jollity that keeps
                us high.
            Have mercy.

Give us a substantial faith.
Even before we call, You are answering
            and You are hearing us right now.
We have been quickened,
nothing delays our rejoicing.
We have been made clean,
a right spirit even now invades our minds
and courses through our veins.
We are strong, on firmest ground, and free.
We have come again to festing and festivities
            radiant with new clothing.
            Smothered with Your kiss of peace.

AN EARTH REDEEMED

When we partake of the living bread and the living vine, our
    triune God,
help us to know ourselves to have part in an earth redeemed;
Help us to know ourselves to have part in new life blood for
    the world:
to cling together as branches to the vine,
to give both shade and refreshment to the world.
Help us to be Thy healing spirit in the world
till all shall be pervaded.
So shall we freshly partake:
So shall we freshly purvey:
So shall we freshly be Thy life of love
till Thou shalt come to judge.

God the Creator, Thou hast made the bread.
Christ the Redeemer, Thou hast changed it.
Holy Spirit, the Binder, Thou dost convey it:
bread for our touching, food for our souls:
Even as lives are bound together in Thee.

God the Creator, Thou hast made the vine.
Christ the Redeemer: Thou hast changed it.
Holy Spirit, the Binder, Thou dost convey it:
the cup from hand to hand, the life blood from heart to
    heart:
Even as our lives are bound together in Thee.

God the Creator, Thou hast changed us.
Christ the Redeemer, Thou hast changed us.
Holy Spirit, the Binder, Thou dost keep us changed:
Even as our lives are bound together in Thee.

LORD OF THE DANCE
(A folk communion)

Indeed it is right . . . what else can we do . . . any time . . . any place . . . than feel uplifted and warmed . . . in our whole being. Father God. What else can we do than feel grateful?

For we remember You, O Christ, the Great Reality . . . the Sun behind all suns: You left Your royal throne . . . left the realm of light . . . to enter our common paths . . . and grope for us in our darkness.
Just for us men . . . common . . . sly . . . and prickly as we are . . . to lift us and soothe us and make us clean.
We cannot put into words . . . but we try to say with our lips what we do believe in our hearts . . . that we really are so grateful . . . that You were born in poverty and not in privilege . . . that You jostled with evil and with filth and never got contaminated.

Lord Jesus, mystical presence of love, we are so grateful that, when all Your sweetness and forbearance went for nothing, You still climbed onto a cross to make us certain You really meant it . . . that for six black hours You danced in agony . . . with the devil on your back, into black night . . . and for six black hours . . . all the evil in the world was confronted by You alone . . . and that, after three days, up came the Sun, King Jesus . . . and You walked and talked again. And the dance went on.

How grateful we are that in the perpetual mystery You are walking and speaking with us now . . . and what You are Lord of is a dance and not a dirge . . . so that we too can dance wherever we may be.

Therefore, with all the powers that go to make the world, all the forces that keep us alive, we sing to You . . . with the whole realm of nature . . . with all the saints . . . with Columba . . . and Kentigern . . . and Ninian . . . who can't really be dead . . . and with all those who used to worship with us on earth, and with our own friends with whom we used to stand in Church, who now, in the mystery still stand beside us, they in Your nearer presence . . . we join with them all singing in our hearts to You ''Holy, holy, holy . . .''

You come to us as we grasp that this bread is vibrant with You, who inhabits all things, and this wine pulsates with You . . . dark with your continuing sacrifice . . . and therefore elixir of our spirits and seal of our right to dance . . .

A TEMPLE FIT

Almighty God, Creator:
In every generation
the rock, the slate, the wood are all fashioned of Thy hand.
And it is also by Thy strength and inspiration
that in every generation rock and slate and wood are shaped
   by hands of men
to make a temple fit for Thee.

Thus: nigh on eight hundred years ago
these walls were fashioned for Thy praise.
But they splintered, mouldered and decayed.
Now they are restored again,
shaped for Thy praise.

Almighty God, Redeemer:
The flesh and blood and bones of each of us
first were framed a temple for Thy spirit.
But they splinter with our sin,
moulder through our neglect.
Our bones, our flesh decay
with the inexorable passing of the years.
Yet they are fashioned by Thee for redemption.

Neither eight hundred years ago, nor yesterday
are these our flesh and bones redeemed;
but now in this moment
as we put our trust in Thee
we are made new.
New creatures we become.
The inner flesh of our immortal bodies—vibrant to eternity.

Almighty God, Sustainer and Controller:
Thy spirit broods again within these walls.
Thy spirit also leaps to flame in each of our spirits
as we put our trust in Thee.
Behold us all together a living temple unto thee.

LESS WORTHY MEMBERS

Lord Christ, Your church is a mystery:
>> It is not a human amalgamation of people trying
>> to be loyal to You.
>> It is not an army of soldiers drilling together to
>> achieve the discipline to be brave.
>> It is not a human list of souls trying sincerely to be
>> good.
It is a mystery of Your own creating:
>> It is Your continuing body on earth:
>> It is flesh of Your flesh and bone of Your bone:
>> It is Your bride.
So there just aren't a lot of churches: because You can't have
a lot of bodies.

So we ask You to open our minds and our hearts next time
we sit at the communion table
to see Baptists and Anglicans: Orthodox and Romans and
Presbyterians all sitting at the same communion table
because that is how You see them:
one body now with You, Your bride, bone of Your bone and
flesh of Your flesh.
Our prayer is that You enlarge our hearts
to serve all Christians with uncalculating love: without
waiting:
even should they spurn us or turn from us.
We thank You for the present unity of the Church.
Help us to go right ahead in the light of it.

Let us pray for the less worthy members of the Church:
They are already limbs of Your mystical body:
forgetful You are already the head, and they the limbs.
Less worthy members who retain signs of their one-time
earthiness:
with continuing prejudices:
all too ready to whisper the damaging libel about their
neighbours:
especially when that libel is true.
All too eager to retell the nasty joke to gain popularity:
forgetting the weaker brethren.

All too tribal, as if Bethlehem were a Scottish village
and Nazareth an English town:
or Capetown were Calvary itself:
when You really died for all men everywhere:
At a crossroads whose signpost had to be in Latin and
   Hebrew and Greek and Urdu and Russian and Afrikaans.
Yes, Lord, we pray for the less worthy members of the
   Church.
They are of course none other than ourselves.

A GREAT MYSTERY IS YOUR CHURCH

Almighty God:
We bless You for the mystery of the Church.
No human society is she, striving to be like You.
No accidental throwing together of struggling humans is she.
She is bone of Your bone and flesh of Your flesh.
She is Your substantiation here on earth.
A great mystery is Your Church.

We did not choose to be Your heralds and to be Your
   defenders.
You chose us: and named us and appointed us to bear fruit.
A great mystery is Your Church.

Nor did You choose us because we are a great people:
It is clear for anyone to see that we are the least of all people.
You have put Your love upon us because You love us—
A great mystery is Your Church.

You are the bread of life: You are the whole loaf.
And we are the particles: we the flour: You the leaven.
A great mystery is Your Church.

You are the vine: not even just the root.
You are the vine and we are the branches.
A great mystery.

You died on Calvary: to rise again and to reign now.
And we were buried with You in the waters of baptism
that with You we might rise to newness of life.
We are already dead, and our lives are hid with You.
The undertakers have been and gone for us.
Our citizenship is already in heaven.
We are just Your ambassadors here
to represent You to a fallen world.
It's all so strange: but You made it like that.

You ordained that You would have no hands now but our
   hands:
No feet but our feet.
Ours are the eyes with which You have ordained
that You look out on the world.
And You are love: uncalculating love.
When we kick You in the teeth,
Your sole concern in whether we have stubbed our toes.
It is all so humiliating . . . and so upbuilding.
You are not a magistrate: just a passionate Father.
Never yearning for us so much as when we go astray.

So help us to forget about denominations.
And each of us: all of us to serve You as You deserve.
We ask it in gratitude and abasement.

38

A CHAOS OF UNCALCULATING LOVE

We are living in a changing day, Lord:
all the old rules and regulations for living
are slithering to the ground.
And You lived in a changing day, Lord:
all the old rules and regulations of the scribes and Pharisees
were slithering to the ground.
But it was Your custom to go to the temple:
to the noisome temple
sometime to the scandalized temple
listening to the mumbo jumbo,
but it was Your custom to go
till the new temple of Your body was available for men.

Give us grace in our changing day
to stand by the temple that is the present church.
The noisome temple
the sometime scandalized temple
that is the present church,
listening sometime to what again seems mumbo jumbo.

Make it our custom to go
till the new outline of Your Body for our day
becomes visible in our midst.

In the temple You healed, Lord Christ:
despite the noise and scandal, You healed.
And we are Your body even today.
You have no hands but our hands
no feet but our feet
ours are the eyes with which You look out
compassionate on the world.

You have ordained that You just don't come
except through us.
Give us faith in great healings
despite the noise and scandal of our modern dimness.
Your grace and power are such:
none can ever ask too much.
Heal again, even through us,
for so You have ordained:
till the new outline of Your body
becomes visible in our midst.

In the temple You threw out the money changers, Lord Christ:
down the steps and out of the door—
and into the vacant aisles came the children
shouting for joy and dancing round.
Too often we are the money changers:
giving short change in spiritual things
to many who seek the true coin:
making the Church an institute
when you want it to be a chaos of uncalculating love.
Drive out from our hearts
our calculated offerings,
our easy responses,
and let child-like faith
flood into us again.
Grant us such abandon, of Your grace alone,
that we too shall be made strong
to go outside the city wall
outside holiness
and die in the bloody mess of another Calvary
that the Church at home may live again.

THE YOUNG LIONS DO LACK AND SUFFER HUNGER: BUT THEY THAT TRUST IN THE LORD SHALL NOT WANT ANYTHING THAT IS GOOD

O God of power, Who didst mightily use this place in ancient days for the saving of thy people: and didst fill so full the hearts of Thy servants here that they went out, caring nothing for their future or their reputation: we thank Thee for the innumerable mercies that have flowed from their sacrifices and pains.

We lift up our hearts in thanksgiving to Thee for the wonder and mystery of Thy Church from that day unto this: ever moving out to do battle: ever recalled to listen to the still small voice.
We thank Thee for the men who first came to these shores in obedience to Thy commands: especially St. Columba and his first community who sallied forth from here and returned for their refreshing.

We praise Thee that a great company are around us as we pray—unknown men lost in coracles on western seas:
humble men of heart apprehended of their sister, Death: on mountain and in forest, just for the love of Thy name.
Compassed about with so great a cloud of witnesses: inspire us to know that Thou art the same today.

Grant grace to the hearts of Thy servants who would renew their vows to Thee.
Grant strength to their bodies: and peace to their souls that caring nothing for their futures or their reputations, they and all of us may be humbled in gratitude:
that by Thee being abased, by Thee they may be exalted, and may go back to their work in the world, renewed, strengthened and at peace, to sail forth together with Thy whole church to the rescue of a shipwrecked world.

Especially we bless Thee that Thou dost gather us in that same faith and in the power of that same spirit:

> that the ancient chain remains unbroken and new links ever forged: unto that perfect day when the chain shall be a circle and all of us together shall surround the everlasting throne.

We are not worthy of those who built Thy church in early days:

> the salt sprays that drenched them
> the waves that engulfed them
> the forests in which they died
> all for the love of Thy name.

Despite the sunlight of faith in which we live—we are so blind.
Despite our smoother passage—we are so hesitant to launch away.
Despite the overflowing knowledge all about us of Thy risen and triumphant power—

> we are so entombed by the doubts of our minds
> and the darkness of our times.

Look down upon us all
Especially we give back to thee

> all our failures to keep our vows
> all our legalisms
> all our despondencies.

Grant, merciful Lord, to all penitent souls both pardon and peace, that we may serve Thee with a quiet mind and unfailingly believe Thy holy gospel.

A TEMPLE NOT MADE WITH HANDS

Lord Jesus, You are above us—reigning.
We believe it.
That is what gives us serenity to achieve.
Years ago there were doubting Thomases.
But this place has been renewed.
And we thank You.

Lord Jesus, You are before us—directing.
We believe it.
That is what gives us courage to go on.
New challenges already beckon and again we sometimes
  dither.
But it is You that directs.
It is You that beckons.
So we dedicate ourselves.
And we bless You.

Lord Jesus, You are beneath us.
We believe it.
When we slip, You catch us.
When we kick You in the face, You just serve us.
And when we pack in and fall right down,
You come further down just to be beside us.
In awe we thank You.

Lord Jesus, You are within each of us.
Our hope of glory, of being complete.
We believe it.
It is not just the interior of these walls:
it's our own inner beings You have renewed.

We are Your temple not made with hands.
We are Your body.
If every wall should crumble, and every church decay,
we are Your habitation.
Nearer are You than breathing, closer than hands and feet.
Ours are the eyes with which You, in the mystery,
look out in compassion on the world.

So we bless You for this place.
For Your directing of us, Your redeeming of us,
and Your indwelling.
Take us "outside the camp", Lord.
Outside holiness.
Out to where soldiers gamble,
and thieves curse,
and nations clash
at the cross-roads of the world.
Maul us up, as You were mauled.
So shall this building continue to be justified.

THE CHURCH AT HOME

Let us pray for our own church,
the place where we were brought up—
the place where we now worship.
Let us remember its achievements.

Children, in all the dross of false teaching,
still clutching the gold;
going about forgiving
because they know they are forgiven;
going about fearless
because they know evil is conquered.

And ourselves,
forgiving and fearless because of what we did learn there,
all the dross swept away.

And old folk not afraid of crossing the bourne,
and sorrowing folk bereaved of dear ones,
but not bitter,
because they know the empty chair
is not empty for always,
because there will be a meeting again.

And young folk,
tempted of passion or of acquisitiveness,
who have been stayed from lust or from dishonesty
because of what they did learn
in the all too faulty fellowship of the church at home.

We bless You, O God, for that church at home.
Let us remember its frailties.
It is often too frail for the modern storm,
is that church at home.
Too conformist to a world that's dying.
Too respectable for the drunkard
or the wretch to feel at home.
Too keen about its money to accuse an acquisitive society.
Too concerned about its own internal peace
to say the scarifying word about the Cross
as the way of peace for the world.

We ask You, Lord,
so to invade that church at home
that it becomes careless of dollars and pounds,
more careful of drunkards
more courageous for peace
more acquisitive of love.

And just because each one of us is that church at home, help
    us to view again
our attitude to money in the light of Your poverty,
our attitude to drunkards and the lecherous in the light of
    Your love for them,
our attitude to war in the light of Your so strange way of
    dealing with it.

Lest, when we speak so critically
of the frailty of our church at home,
in our walks we should confront You, Lord Christ,
suddenly at the bend of the road
and not escape Your silent gaze at us
Your silent gaze at each one of us
so clearly saying:

"You are the cause of the frailty of the church at home."

BY GRACE INVADE US

Lord Jesus Christ in the upper room:
they were moody, having quarrelled—
which would be greatest?
and Thou didst take a towel
and began to wash their feet.
Behold us all in this place:
too often moody about this thing,
in tension as to which road to Thee has surest foundation.
Lord Jesus, look up to each of us
as in patience still Thou dost wash our feet.

Lord Jesus Christ:
in the upper room Thou didst pray
that they all might be one
that the world might believe.
And that we might be one
that the world might believe.
And the world does not believe . . . multitudes of them.
Yea Lord, the little world around each of us does not even
    believe.
Some because of their pride . . . do not believe.
Some because of lust of body or of wealth . . . do not
    believe.
But some do not believe because we are not one.

There are too often moody Presbyterians
persistent that they shall not let their fathers down:
Lazy even to consider what their fathers might have said.

There are Roman Catholics callous in their calamitous claim
that only they can know. Deaf even to listen
to what their closest brothers now attempt to plead.

There are Anglicans so bedevilled to be a bridge
that they are blind to the splitting timbers at either end
that might make their bridge an island.

And everyone of us here, from time to time,
lazy, deaf and blind as any of them.

Look up to us, look up to each of us
as in humility still
Thou dost wash our feet.

By grace invade us once again, each of us
with the knowledge that though Thy bones are out of joint
not one of them is broken.
Disjointed by our sin: not one of them is broken.
Invade us once again, each of us,
with the knowledge that we have part in Thee.
Invade us with the awful knowledge
that we have only part in Thee as we let Thee wash our feet.
Invade us with the wondrous knowledge
that if Thou dost wash our feet
we are clean every whit.

Rejoice us with the signs of lowly unity.
Rejoice us that there are Roman Catholics prepared to face
    obloquy
that unity may be seen.
There are Anglicans suspect and shunned
that unity may be seen.
There are Presbyterians blackguarded
that unity may be seen.
Lowly men of heart
whom even now in the secret coronation Thou dost crown
that the world may believe.

WHERE FREEDOM IS, AND LAUGHTER

It's not my brother nor my sister but it's me, O Lord:
standing in the need of prayer.
We are so warm in our own self esteem
that we freeze the folk around us.
We get so high in our own estimation
that we stand isolated on a mountain top of self
    righteousness.
That is why You came: Lord Jesus:
not to save the lecherous but to turn the righteous to
    repentance.
And it is me, O Lord.

It is just not true, Lord Jesus,
that if we had lived with You we would have turned.
The disciples lived with You,
heard Your words,
saw Your wonders,
dined with You and wined with You
and for two years were bathed in Your unspeakable grace.
Yet when You asked them to wait with You for one hour
they all fell asleep.
So You just had to climb on that cross
on the day the sun refused to shine.
So we confess we can't make it.
And most certainly we can't take it.
So we ask You to make us new.
You alone are in right relations with the Father.
Only in You can we be in right relations with anyone.
Give us grace not to try to go it alone.
Give us grace to go along with You:
where freedom is, and laughter:
legalities are swallowed up in love:
and no one is to blame
because You have taken it all yourself.
Jesus Lord and Saviour. It is so.

CHILDREN OF CONFUSION

Living and eternal God:
Indeed Thou hast recorded Thy name here on this spot.
From year to year
from century to century
in Celtic praise
in Roman chant
in hymns of later days
Thy salvation has been declared
Thy name has been adored.
From these shores have gone missionaries of the cross
crusaders of the faith.

Now in our day, led of Thy spirit
we come from close-built city
from country town
from factory, bank, and university
seeking the same salvation Thou hast always offered.
We of this day are not children of the faith:
rather are we children of confusion.
The noise of cities deafens us
to the still small voice.
The pace of modern living blurs for us
the vision beautiful.
The pride of learning darkens the light of the eternal word:
children of confusion.
But Thou that knowest our infirmities still dost call us here:
Thou rememberest our frame.
It must be us whom Thou desirest to invade for Thee the
    cities,
to confront the factories,
new missionaries of the cross.
We are not worthy
but our sufficiency is in Thee.
We thank Thee for new insights into Thy word,
for tasks more clearly seen,
for deepened consciousness of the power of Christian
    fellowship.
And so in confidence
we ask Thee to go before us
back to the city—

back to the counter and the bench,
the better instruments for Thy using
because we know ourselves so weak that we must turn to Thee.

CHANGE OUR HABITS AND OUR LIVES

Let us pray for the recovery of prophecy:
Almighty God who in Thy holy word has commanded Thy prophets to walk warily in times of peace and boldly in times of trouble, inspire all who speak where many listen or write what many read, with great boldness at the present time.
Help them to proclaim without fear the full Christian gospel according as they read Thy word.

Let us pray for all believers in their vocation and ministry:
Almighty God who hast called all believers to a full vocation, so that Thy priesthood is in every home and place of work, we lift to Thee Thy ministers at factory bench, at desk, in kitchen and wherever a witness can be made.
Visit them in their times of prayer, that all who work beside them may take note that they have been with Jesus, and by the standard that they see in them may be rebuked or comforted till they seek of us and of them our secret as it is in Thee.

Let us pray for believers in their family circle:
Almighty God, Who hast set us in families so that we may understand Thy fatherhood in the great family of the Church: we pray for all who seek to make place for Thee at the hearths of home.
Open Thy word again in the houses of our people, inspire parents to lead and to teach the young in prayer, that the daily worship of our land may ascend from every Christian home, and Thy sufficiency be known again in things both great and small.

Let us pray for a new social order:
O King Who wilt not reign save by election of Thy citizens, we do exalt Thee to the throne of our affairs and offer our allegiance to Thy government in all our ways of life.
Bind up the world's wounds, that ours also may be healed for the sake of Him who bore the sins of all mankind, and therefore ours. Forgive our guilty share of all the evil that is done on earth.
Change Thou our habits and our lives that society may be transformed. And let a saved community bear witness to our souls' salvation.

WE FRAIL CREATURES OF A PASSING DAY

Almighty and everlasting: God of our fathers
Guide unto our children's children.
We the frail creatures of a passing day
Come once more in Thy presence
to renew our vows unto Thee
and to ask Thee, unworthy though we be,
to renew for us Thy presence.

We confess we cannot live without Thy presence.
Life is too hard for us and duty too large.
We do seek to serve Thee but the feeble hands hang down:
We try to worship, but how soon do our minds wander . . .
And as we falter and ponder we know
it is because too often we are neglectful of Thy kindness
and scornful of Thy power.

So often in the hymns we sing we call Thee King: and how
    rebellious we are.
So easily we call thee Master: and how unprofitable we are.
Daily we call Thee Father: and we are so disobedient.

Especially we remember those sins
that are the present burden of our minds . . .
Grant merciful Father, to all penitent souls
Thy pardon and Thy peace
that they may serve Thee with a quiet mind.

Keep us in the constant sense of Thy presence and
    forgiveness
that, going our way with gladness,
we may come at last to these things
which eye hath not seen nor ear heard
but which Thou hast prepared
for all of them that love Thee
from the foundations of the world.

57

THE STEEPNESS OF THE BRAE

Lord, have mercy
Christ have mercy
Lord have mercy.
Yea Lord, have mercy.
We know Thou art the way for us:
But we do not like the steepness of the brae.
We know Thou art the truth for us:
But we do not like the starkness of Thy word.
We know Thou art the life for us:
But still we fear that days would be dull
or too demanding
if we gave up ours.
And even though we know Thou hast climbed the brae,
taken the starkness from the truth,
and the sweat from the demand,
we still stand, and fear, and hesitate . . .

Wilt Thou not turn again and quicken us
that Thy people may rejoice in Thee?
Make me a clean heart, O God
and renew a right spirit within me.
O give me the comfort of Thy help again
and establish me with Thy free spirit.

Yea Lord, establish us with Thy free spirit:
The hill is conquered—Calvary is bare.
The truth has triumphed—the tomb is empty.
Life is abundant—the Law is dead.

Thou hast renewed a right spirit within us.
Thou hast turned again and we are quickened.
Even that which we have asked for—
we believe that we have it.
Really and truly we believe Thy whole good news.
Behold us: Thy people who now rejoice in Thee.

A VEIL THIN AS GOSSAMER

Be Thou, triune God, in the midst of us as we give thanks for those who have gone from the sight of earthly eyes. They, in Thy nearer presence, still worship with us in the mystery of the one family in heaven and on earth.

We remember those whom Thou didst call to high office, as the world counts high. They bore the agony of great decisions and laboured to fashion the Ark of the Covenant nearer to Thy design.

We remember those who, little recognised in the sight of men, bore the heat and burden of the unrecorded day. They served serene because they knew Thou hadst made them priests and kings, and now shine as the stars forever.

If it be Thy holy will, tell them how we love them, and how we miss them, and how we long for the day when we shall meet with them again.

God of all comfort, we lift into Thine immediate care those recently bereaved, who sometimes in the night time cry "would God it were morning", and in the morning cry "would God it were night." Bereft of their dear ones, too often they are bereft also of the familiar scenes where happiness once reigned.

Lift from their eyes the too distant vision of the resurrection at the last day. Alert them to hear the voice of Jesus saying "I AM Resurrection and I AM Life": that they may believe this.

Strengthen them to go on in loving service of all Thy children. Thus shall they have communion with Thee and, in Thee, with their beloved. Thus shall they come to know, in themselves, that there is no death and that only a veil divides, thin as gossamer.

THE GALILEAN LANGUAGE

Let us pray for the peace of the world. Prayer is the same word as pray-er, Lord. You can't begin to answer us till we are the words we pray. We would like fair shares for all round the world, and no one starving and no one cold. And You are the bread of life and can do it through us. But Your life was giving; and how much of ours is keeping. We must have our gadgets; we must have our lushness, our holidays, our balances, our superiority, our surpluses. So nothing much happens about the starving and the cold. Our 2 percent providings and our 98 percent prerogatives. "Give us this day our daily bread" hardly spans our own local river, scarcely begins to embrace the poverty accumulating on the Red Sea shore. Give us Pentecost, Lord, where Jews and Arabs, Africans and Afrikaners, Germans, Russians, and Chinese begin to listen once again just to the Galilean language.

We would like to be rid of armaments, Lord. Everyone would like to be rid of armaments—Jews, Arabians, Greeks, and Chinese. But it's "what other chaps might do," say the Greeks, say the Arabs, say the Jews, say the Chinese. And, dear Lord, we say it too.

Come into our council chambers when all the doors are locked. Come in and show us Your broken hands and wounded side as at the first Easter. Say again with power, "Peace be unto you." And take us back to Galilee for a great catch. Give us a Pentecost again, so that all of us can hear the Galilean language.

Take us to the mountaintop today. Dear Lord, convince us of Your radiant body, alive with light and pouring out its freshness from above to radiate the whole round world. But recall us to our allegiance. We are the only radiant body that You have got. If love does not start with us, it will never start at all. Pentecost is not some future hope. The rushing, mighty wind of peace is howling to get into the shuttered, fetid prison we have contrived, buttressed by our prejudices, barred and bolted with our fears. Give us faith in peace again, faith in Your way of peace. It will never come from the Vatican or bishops or assemblies. It will only come from You to each. It can only come through each of us right now. Take the terror from us. Give us faith.

Or failing that—give us the honesty not to pray to You for peace at all. We ask it for Your sake indeed.

ACKNOWLEDGEMENTS

Photographs by

Anna Briggs   page 33

Duncan Finlayson   page 63

Geoff Houghton   Cover
                             and pages 9, 12, 15, 23, 28,
                             35, 37, 39, 42, 44, 48, 51, 53,
                             55, 57, 61

Michael Lee   pages 30, 59

Don Stubbings   pages 18, 20, 26